DISCOVERING

◆

JapaN

By Deborah Tyler

CRESTWOOD HOUSE
New York

A ZOË BOOK

© 1993 Zoë Books Limited

First American publication 1993 by Crestwood House, Macmillan Publishing Company, 866 Third Avenue, New York, NY 10022

Macmillan Publishing Company is part of the Maxwell Communication Group of Companies.

First published in Great Britain in 1993 by
Zoë Books Limited
15 Worthy Lane
Winchester
Hampshire SO23 7AB

Devised and produced by
Zoë Books Limited
15 Worthy Lane
Winchester
Hampshire SO23 7AB

Printed in Italy by Grafedit SpA
Design: Jan Sterling, Sterling Associates
Picture research: Suzanne Williams
Map: Gecko Limited
Production: Grahame Griffiths

8 7 6 5 4 3 2 1

Library of Congress Cataloging-in-Publication Data

Tyler, Deborah.
    Japan / by Deborah Tyler.
    p. cm. — (Discovering)
    Includes index.
    Summary: A look at one of the most industrialized nations and how it has changed over the years. Includes information about the economy, lifestyle and history of Japan.
    ISBN 0-89686-773-0
    1. Spain — Juvenile literature. [1. Spain.]
DS806.T95. 1993
952— dc20   93-3268

Photographic acknowledgments
The publishers wish to acknowledge, with thanks, the following photographic sources:

Cover: Zefa; title page: Robert Harding Picture Library/Rolf Richardson; 5l Robert Harding Picture Library/Carol Jopp; 5r Robert Harding Picture Library/Nigel Blythe; 6 Robert Harding Picture Library; 7l The Hutchison Library/Jon Burbank; 7r Zefa; 8 Impact Photos/Michael Gover; 9l,9r,10 Zefa; 11t Werner Forman Archive/Burke Collection, New York; 11b Michael Holford; 12 The Hutchison Library/Michael MacIntyre; 13l The Hutchison Library; 13r Robert Harding Picture Library/Paul van Riel; 14 Robert Harding Picture Library/Nigel Blythe; 15l David Lewis; 15r Impact Photos/Mark Cator; 16 Robert Harding Picture Library; 17l The Hutchison Library/Jon Burbank; 17r Robert Harding Picture Library/Robert McLeod; 18 Impact Photos/Mark Cator; 19l Robert Harding Picture Library; 19r The Hutchison Library; 20 Zefa; 21l The Hutchison Library/R.Ian Lloyd; 21r Robert Harding Picture Library/Robert McLeod; 22 The Hutchison Library/Jon Burbank; 23tl Zefa; 23bl & r Robert Harding Picture Library; 24 Zefa; 25l The Hutchison Library/Jon Burbank; 25r Robert Harding Picture Library; 26 Syndication International; 27l & r The Hutchison Library/Michael MacIntyre; 28 Roger Ressmeyer, Starlight/Science Photo Library; 29l The Hutchison Library; 29r Nasda/Science Photo library.

Cover: *Mount Fuji*

Title page: *The Ginza area of Tokyo, at night*

Contents

Yookoso   5

People, language and customs   6

Traveling in Japan   8

Emperors and shoguns   10

Kyoto and Tokyo   12

Living in Japan   14

Food and shopping   16

Education and work   18

Japan—the industrial giant   20

Holidays and festivals   22

Religion   24

Japan at war   26

A changing world   28

Fact file   30

Index   32

4

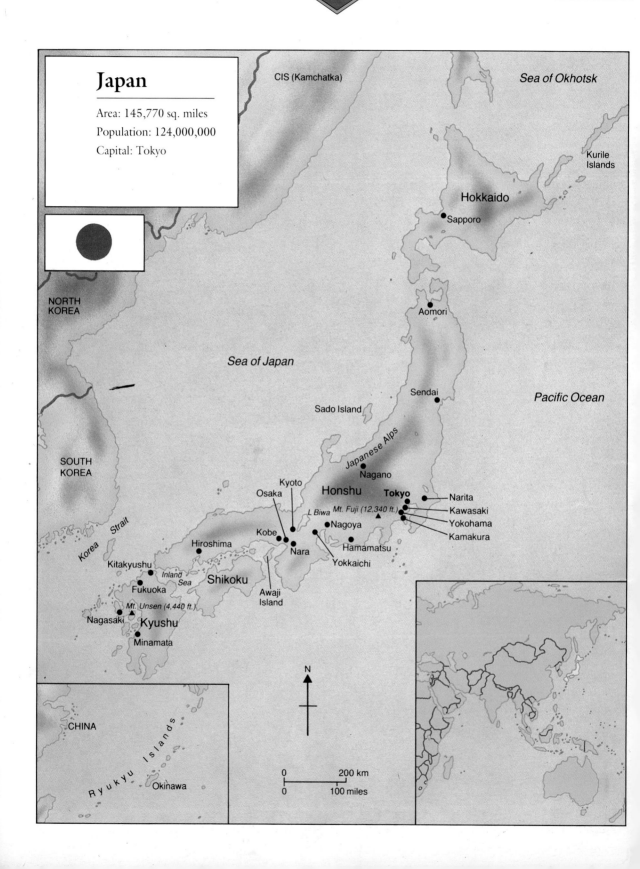

Yookoso ようこそ

Welcome to Japan. Japan is called Nippon, or Land of the Rising Sun, by the Japanese. It is in the western part of the Pacific Ocean. As the sun rises in Japan, people in Great Britain are finishing dinner and New Yorkers are still at work.

There are about 4,000 islands in Japan. Some are too small for people to live on. The mainland is made up of the four largest islands—Hokkaido, Honshu, Shikoku and Kyushu. Japan is not a small country. It stretches nearly 2,000 miles from north to south. Most of the land is wooded mountains with narrow valleys. The Japanese Alps on Honshu form a barrier 10,000 feet high between the Pacific coast and the Sea of Japan.

Because most people have to live on the areas of flat land by the coasts or in the valleys, some parts of Japan are very crowded. The largest area of flat

Cherry blossom viewing parties are held in spring.

land is the Kanto plain, around the capital city, Tokyo. Hokkaido has about 25 percent of the land area of Japan, but only 5 percent of the population live there.

Climate

Japan has distinct seasons. The north and the mountains have snow in winter. Spring is mild and brings the plum, peach and cherry blossoms so loved by the Japanese. Summer is hot and humid. The countryside is very green because rain is plentiful in the growing season. In autumn the maple leaves and chrysanthemums bring brilliant color.

Autumn colors in the mountains

People, language and customs

Nearly all the people living in Japan are Japanese. Only about 1 percent of the population are non-Japanese. There are about 70,000 Koreans and about 150,000 Chinese. Thousands of workers, mainly from Asia, come to Japan to find jobs, but they are not allowed to stay long.

Language

There are many differences between the English language and Japanese. In Japanese there is no word for *a* or *the*, and there is no plural form. For example, the word for *child* can mean one child or lots of children. Some words and phrases in Japanese can be spoken only by men. Others are only used by women.

A foreigner learning Japanese must be careful not to use the wrong ones! There are also different forms to show politeness and respect.

Japanese and English—mixed

Many English words have been borrowed by the Japanese. They sound so different in Japanese that English speakers do not always recognize them. Some examples are *orenji jusu* (orange juice), *sandoicchi* (sandwich), *bijinesuman* (businessman). All Japanese learn English at school for six years. They learn to read English, but they do not often speak it.

Both kana and kanji can be seen on these Tokyo street signs.

A lesson in writing kanji

Writing

The first writing in Japan was Chinese, using characters known as kanji. This is a way of writing the meaning of a word with a sign rather like a picture. Japanese is very different from Chinese. Japanese has more sounds. A kanji can be spoken in many different ways in Japanese. By about A.D. 900 the Japanese had worked out a system to write the sounds of their own language. Japanese is still written using this mixed system. Schoolchildren must learn 1,945 kanji and two sets of symbols, or kana. Each kana has 46 signs. Japanese is usually written from top to bottom, beginning on the right.

Giving gifts

The giving of gifts is an important custom in Japan. At midyear and at the end of the year, everyone gives gifts to say thank you to bosses, people at work and neighbors. People give presents for birthdays, visits and other occasions, too. It is considered polite to wrap presents. Shops have special departments selling gifts prettily packed in boxes. Money is put in special envelopes tied with ribbon. For New Year's, weddings and other celebrations, the ribbons are red or gold. For funerals they are silver or black. On St. Valentine's Day (February 14), girls give chocolate. A month later, on White Day, boys give white chocolates.

Names

In Japanese, a family name, or surname, comes first, then the given name, or first name. Only family and friends use a given name.

Bowing

Japanese people bow when they meet each other, and when they say good-bye, sorry or thank you. Mothers teach small children to bow. At school and at work, people learn even more rules about bowing. It becomes such a habit that some people even bow when they are talking on the telephone.

Shopping for gifts

Traveling in Japan

People drive cars on the left in Japan. Traffic jams in the big cities are often very bad. In Tokyo they can spread up to 30 miles. The Japanese motor companies make a special system for their cars. Information from satellites and boxes beside the main roads warn drivers of traffic jams ahead.

About 12 million people live in Tokyo and another 3 million come in each day to work. In order to encourage commuters to use public transportation, the city charges high parking fees. Most people walk or cycle to their local station and travel by train. Trains are very crowded during the rush hour, and many people have to stand. Marks on the platform show exactly where the doors will be. Travelers know where to wait so they can get on quickly.

Trains and boats

Private railroad lines link the suburbs and Japan's main city centers. Some of the lines run underground. The main railway company is the Japan Railways Group, or JR. It runs 26,000 trains a day over 13,000 miles of track on the four main islands. Some of the trains are double-

Rush hour in Tokyo

deckers. The more expensive seats, each with its own TV, are on the top deck. Signs are written in Japanese and English at all JR stations.

Before the railroads were built in Japan, just over 100 years ago, the easiest way to travel was by boat. Ferries still cross the Inland Sea and link all the islands. The six largest cities in Japan are all on the coast.

Bullet trains

The fastest trains are the *shinkansen*, or "bullet trains." These trains travel at 170 miles per hour. The first line was built for the Olympic Games in 1964, to link Tokyo with Osaka, 343 miles away. There are now four lines. A Japanese company is trying out new "maglev" trains. These trains have no wheels but are pulled along a special track using power from magnets. Maglev trains will be able to travel as fast as 310 miles per hour.

The bullet train passing Mount Fuji

Tunnels and bridges

Many of the islands are linked by bridges. The bridge connecting Shikoku to Okayama on Honshu is the world's

Kobe city harbor

longest road-rail bridge. By 1997 the world's longest suspension bridge will be completed, linking Kobe to Awaji island.

There are also tunnels under the sea. The longest tunnel is 33.5 miles long, called the Seikan Tunnel. This tunnel links Honshu with the island of Hokkaido.

Air travel

There are 60 airports in Japan and three Japanese airlines. A monorail links Haneda Airport to the center of Tokyo—for flights within Japan. The New International Airport is at Narita, 37 miles north of Tokyo. In Osaka Bay an international airport is being built on an artificial island. When it opens in 1994, speedboats will take passengers to Kobe in less than 30 minutes.

The red crane

The symbol of Japan Airlines (JAL) is a red crane. There are many symbols in Japanese art. A crane means good fortune. These birds are protected. About 400 of them live wild on Hokkaido.

Emperors and shoguns

The Todaiji temple at Nara

Over 12,000 years ago, Stone Age people called the Ainu lived in Japan. Other peoples began to move into Japan from northeast Asia and southern China. The Ainu were pushed northward. Today about 24,000 Ainu people still live on Hokkaido. The earliest records about Japan are 1,700 years old. The writers described a country with women rulers.

The first capital

No one is sure of the date of the first emperor, but the emperors and empresses of Japan have come from one family for at least 1,500 years. The court used to move to each new emperor's home. In A.D. 710, the people who helped rule the country decided to stay in one place. They built a capital at Heijokyo, or Capital of the Peaceful Fortress. This city is now called Nara. After 75 years, an emperor named Kammu decided that the religious leaders had become too powerful. He built a new capital a few miles away from the temples of Nara at Heian-kyo, or Capital of Peace. This new city was the capital for nearly 400 years and became known as Kyoto.

Time in Japanese history

Each period of time in Japanese history has a name. At first these periods had the names of the place of government, like Nara. Since 1868 the government has stayed in Tokyo, and historical periods are now named after each emperor instead.

Many shoguns came from the Tokugawa family. This screen shows their castle in Kyoto.

The shoguns

For many years different clans, or family groups, fought for power in Japan. One of these clans was the Genji. In the 1100s their leader, Yoritomo, and his army beat the other clans. He was the most powerful man in Japan, and he set up a military government in the town of Kamakura. For 700 years the emperors' court stayed in Kyoto, but the military leaders, or shoguns, ruled the country from their castles.

Isolation

The first Europeans came to Japan in the 1500s. They were Spanish missionaries and Dutch and Portuguese traders. The shoguns did not like the ideas of these foreign people and were afraid of losing their power to them. In 1603 the Tokugawa shoguns ordered that no one could visit Japan and no Japanese could travel abroad without permission. Japan was closed for over 200 years. In 1854 an officer in the U.S. Navy, Commodore Matthew Perry, persuaded the shoguns to open Japanese ports for trade. By 1868 the shoguns had lost power. The emperor moved from Kyoto to the Tokugawa castle at Edo (now Tokyo). A new government was set up.

Portuguese merchants and missionaries arriving in Japan

Kyoto and Tokyo

Tokyo is the capital of Japan today, but Kyoto was the capital for over 1,000 years before that. The Japanese names for the two cities are both written with two characters. The character for *kyo*, which means "capital," appears in each name.

Kyoto

Kyoto was the home of the emperors of Japan for over 1,000 years. The emperor Kammu built the city on a site with hills on three sides for safety. The roads in Kyoto form a grid pattern copied from the ancient capital of China, Ch'ang-on. Kyoto became a center for religion, arts and crafts. Today Kyoto is the seventh largest city in Japan, with a population of over 1.4 million. It is still a center for religion but also has large electrical and chemical industries.

Crafts in Kyoto

There are 1,600 Buddhist temples and 270 Shinto shrines in Kyoto. They were decorated by skilled crafts workers with carved wood and sculptures in stone and bronze. Artists also came to Kyoto to work for the emperor and rich families. They painted screens and fans and copied beautiful Chinese characters onto rolls of paper. The art of fine writing, or calligraphy, is learned by many Japanese today. It takes many years to learn.

The "crane dance" at Yasaka Shrine in Kyoto

A performance of Bunraku in Tokyo

Japanese theater

The four types of theater enjoyed by the court in Kyoto are still popular in Japan. No and kyogen are 600 years old. No is part song and part dance. The rhyming words are chanted by actors wearing masks. Kyogen plays are short comedies. The name means "crazy speech." Bunraku and Kabuki started 400 years ago. Bunraku is a puppet show. The puppeteers train for 30 years. Three men move each puppet. Kabuki began as a religious dance by nuns. Women were banned from working in the theater, so men took the roles. They dress up as women.

Tokyo

Tokyo means "eastern capital." The city was called Edo until the emperor moved there from Kyoto in 1868. The old shoguns' castle became the Imperial Palace, and Tokyo became the capital of Japan.

Edo was once a fishing village on the Sumida River. Three roads met there, and in the 1400s a local lord built a castle to control the people who used the roads. About 150 years later, Ieyasu, the first shogun of the Tokugawa family, made Edo the center of his government. Fifty years later more people lived in Edo than in any other city in the world.

The Imperial Palace and much of Tokyo was destroyed during World War II. Most of the old buildings were wooden. New buildings are made of concrete. Tokyo is now a vast city. It is the center of politics, finance, government, fashion and art. Nearly 25 percent of the population of Japan lives in Greater Tokyo and the port of Yokohama. Under an improvement plan, the government hopes to move some businesses and government departments to less crowded parts of Japan.

The new town hall at Shinjuku, Tokyo

Living in Japan

After World War II many homes had been destroyed and new ones had to be built quickly. There was not much money and not much space in the cities, so most Japanese homes are small. Even in the country, houses only have tiny gardens.

Inside the home

Every home has an entrance hall, or *genkan*, that is lower than the level of the main floor. Outdoor shoes are left in the *genkan*. The main room may have tatami mats made from rice straw on the floor. Sliding screens can divide the room for different uses.

Bedding is kept in cupboards during the day and laid on the floor at night. If children have separate bedrooms, they often sleep in bunk beds to save space.

A family meal at home

Most homes have air conditioners for the summer. On winter evenings the family sits around a low table, a *kotatsu*, to keep warm. There is electric heating under the table and a thick quilt around the sides to keep out drafts.

Baths and slippers

No one wears shoes in a Japanese house. Slippers are kept in the *genkan*. Special plastic slippers are worn in the toilets. This is always in a separate room and never in the bathroom. A Japanese bath is hot and deep. You shower first, outside the bath, and then get in to relax.

Leisure

Sports are popular in Japan, as they are in most places in the world, and nearly every home has a television. There are also some pastimes, however, that are

particularly Japanese, like pachinko and *karaoke*. People in other parts of the world are borrowing some of these leisure pursuits. Although there isn't much time for leisure in Japan, "mind gyms" are becoming very popular with city workers. People lie on gently moving chairs, and listen to special relaxing music on headphones.

Pachinko and *karaoke*

Pachinko is a type of pinball game. Pachinko parlors have bright lights and loud music. They are usually full. Players sit in rows in front of machines and pull handles. Sometimes they win a lot of money.

Many people relax after work in *karaoke* bars. *Karaoke* means "empty orchestra." People use a microphone and take turns singing to prerecorded music.

A pachinko parlor

Baseball practice in Tokyo

Sports

Baseball is a very popular game. There are two professional leagues, each with six teams. They play matches from April to October. Baseball is played at school, and nearly everyone watches the final of the high school contest in August on television. Baseball fields are smaller than usual because of lack of space. For the same reason, golfers have to practice in multistory golf ranges.

Sumo—the national sport

Sumo wrestling is Japan's national sport. It is at least 1,700 years old. At first, contests were held in Shinto shrines. Even today the referee dresses as a Shinto priest. Six tournaments are held each year. It is hard to get tickets, but the contests are shown on television. There are 800 professional wrestlers who train from the age of 15. Sumo wrestlers eat a special diet to become very large. Their average weight is 336 pounds!

Food and shopping

A Japanese meal usually includes rice. The Japanese word for breakfast means "morning rice." Lunch is "noon rice" and dinner is "evening rice." Most homes have electric rice steamers. Rice is also made into cakes for special occasions and into sake, a rice wine.

The Japanese eat a lot of fish, which is often eaten raw. They also eat seaweed. Hardly any meat is eaten, partly because there is very little grassland for sheep or cows. The first Buddhists in Japan were vegetarians. They did not eat meat, so meals without meat are a tradition in Japan. Most Japanese meals include protein obtained from soybeans. Soybeans are made into soy sauce, tofu (bean curd) and miso (soup). A traditional Japanese breakfast consists of rice with raw egg, dried fish, pickles, miso and seaweed. Many Japanese now eat cereal, toast with jam, and coffee for breakfast.

Eating out

The Japanese do not often invite people to their homes for meals. They take guests out to restaurants. The whole family goes out to eat, since Japanese children are not usually left at home with baby-sitters. Before eating, diners are given hot towels to wipe their hands. Then everyone says *itadakimasu*, which means "thank you for the food."

Plastic copies of meals for sale are displayed in the restaurant window.

A family meal of sashimi (raw fish)

Sushi or noodles

Most eating places sell one type of food. You can tell which sort by the writing on the curtains hanging over the door. Sushi bars, for example, sell dishes of raw fish. Some bars are very small. The cook puts dishes onto a conveyor belt in the kitchen. Customers sit at a long counter and take the dish they want as it passes by. Noodle shops sell two types of noodles, *soba* and *udon*. They are served with soup, to eat there or take away.

Street sellers

Street stalls, called *yatai*, sell freshly cooked food. The city of Fukuoka is called the *yatai* capital of Japan. Every evening 230 food stalls are rolled onto the streets. Each town or village also has vending machines on the streets for food, drink and almost anything else!

Shopping

Most shops are open from 10 A.M. to 7 P.M. They are open on Saturdays and Sundays, too, but each shop closes one day a week. Some food shops open 24 hours a day.

In large cities there are underground shopping streets. The railroad companies also build shops over their stations to be used by travelers. The company makes money from the train fares and from the shops. Big department stores, or *depato*, not only sell things but also run evening classes and hold art exhibitions. On the top floor there is usually a doctor, a dentist and a garden, or even rooftop tennis.

Shopping at a market stall in Tokyo

Education and work

Students at Central Tokyo Junior High School

All Japanese children must go to school for nine years, from the age of 6. Nearly all 15-year-olds then go on to senior high school. About half the children who finish high school then go to a college or university, so Japanese workers have a good education. They learn to work hard as soon as they start school.

Exam pressure

Passing exams is very important in Japan. Some children start taking exams at age 3 to go to the best kindergartens. Schools and universities have their own entrance exams. It is important to choose the best place to study, as students from school or university often help one another get good jobs later on.

School day

The school year in Japan starts and ends in the spring. Children start the day at 8:30 A.M. and leave at 3:30 P.M. They go to school on Saturdays, too, but leave earlier, and on one Saturday each month there are sports instead of lessons. There is no school on Sundays.

Prayers for good luck in examinations, placed at a shrine

Juku

After school most children go to clubs or to *juku*. At these private schools they have extra lessons to help them pass exams. At clubs they may play baseball or learn to play a musical instrument. When they get home, they still have two to three hours of homework to do.

Martial arts

Many children learn the traditional Japanese sports at *juku*. These martial arts, or *ninja*, are the skills of the samurai warriors who fought for the emperors and the shoguns. Practice begins with quiet meditation. Students learn self-control as well as self-defense. The martial arts are kendo (fencing), *kyudo* (archery), aikido, judo and karate (self-defense with no weapons).

Work

People starting work with big companies in Japan begin their new jobs on April 1. For the first two weeks they learn about the company. They are taught how to behave and how to bow. In many offices and factories the day begins with exercises. Workers bow to one another and sing their company song.

Most people in Japan work long hours, six days a week. They may have to travel about two hours from home to work. Many husbands spend so long at work and in traveling to and from work that they are known at home as "the boarder." Doctors think *karooshi*, death from overwork, is becoming a serious problem.

Businessmen doing their daily exercises

Women

In Japan few women with children have jobs outside the home. Japanese women used to marry before they were 25 years old. Unmarried women over 25 were called *kurisumasu keki*, or "Christmas Cake"—no good after December 25! Now many women have good jobs and prefer to marry later.

Japan—the industrial giant

Japan is one of the most important industrial nations in the world. Most homes in the United States and Europe have some products made by Japanese companies. Famous names like Sony, Honda, Toshiba and Toyota sell their electrical goods, cars, bicycles, cameras and computers all over the world.

Kyushu is known as Car Island. Nearly 200 factories on the island make parts for cars. Nissan and Toyota make 800,000 cars a year in Fukuoka and Miyata. People in factories at Toyota City on Honshu make four million cars a year.

Robots

Robots are used in many factories around the world. There are now nearly 300,000 of them at work in Japan. The first robots were designed in the United States more than 40 years ago, but Japan now leads the world in developing robots.

Pollution

Pollution is a serious problem in Japan. For example, fishing is forbidden at Minamata, on Kyushu, since 300 people died after eating fish caught in the bay. For many years, the Chisso Corporation pumped waste mercury from its factories into the sea there. In 1992, damages of 578 million yen were paid to 88 people suffering from "Minamata disease." This illness was caused by the Showa Denko Company emptying waste water that contained mercury into a river.

Farming and fishing

Rice plants first came to Japan from China nearly 2,000 years ago. Growing rice is hard work, but the plants produce over 12 million tons a year because the climate and soil are suitable. Although

The Mazda car plant at Hiroshima

Rice fields in northern Honshu

rice has long been an important crop in Japan, more vegetables than rice are grown today.

More farm work is done by hand in Japan than in the United States or Europe. For example, each apple on the trees in the Aomori district of Honshu has a bag over it to guard against frost and birds. Except on Hokkaido, most farms are tiny, often just 2.5 acres. Few farms have full-time workers. Most farming families also work in the cities.

People on fishing boats catch sardines, herring and anchovies around the Japanese coast, but the fishing fleet also goes as far as the Arctic and Antarctica. The Japanese catch more fish throughout the world than any people.

Resources

Japan has plenty of water and trees but little else that is needed for industry. Almost all the raw materials needed to make the goods in the factories have to be imported. Iron ore for steel making comes from Australia, Brazil and India.

Energy

Energy is needed to power machines and to run factories and cars. Water provides some hydroelectric power but only a small part of Japan's total energy needs. Japan's major source of energy is oil, which it imports from the Middle East, Southeast Asia, Mexico and China. There are some coal mines on Hokkaido and Kyushu, but Japan has only about 10 percent of the coal it needs. Japan is the world's largest importer of coal, which it buys mainly from Australia, the United States and Canada.

There are 39 nuclear reactors in Japan that produce electricity. Many people fear accidents at these power stations, remembering the nuclear bombs that fell on Hiroshima and Nagasaki. There is strong opposition to plans to build another 16 of these stations.

Unloading fish at Fukue Island

Holidays and festivals

Although schools close for six weeks in the summer, many office workers have only two weeks vacation a year. There are also 13 national holidays in Japan. The first week in May is called Golden Week because three holidays come close together. Trains, planes and hotels are very full then. New Year's is another busy time, as most offices close for a week. The Japanese like to take vacations abroad, but they do not have much time. Most couples do find time for a honeymoon and often spend a lot of money on a week's special vacation abroad.

Beaches, hot springs and skiing

The beaches near big cities are crowded on summer Sundays. Seaside resorts are quite new in Japan. Many people still prefer to relax in *onsen*, hot spring resorts in the mountains. There are 20,000 *onsen* in Japan. Even in winter some visitors sit in the hot outdoor pools. The mountains are also popular for skiing. Fast trains take skiers to the Japanese Alps during the weekends. About 20 million Japanese go skiing in Nagano every year. There are also ski resorts on Hokkaido.

Festivals

Most towns and villages in Japan have their own special festivals or parades at certain times of the year. In August most people celebrate *o-bon*, a festival for the dead. Their ancestors are important to the Japanese. People travel to their hometowns. They light.bonfires outside their houses to welcome the spirits of dead family members and leave food on their graves. Paper lanterns light the streets for dancing.

Families on the beach in the summer

The hot spring resort at Takaragawa

National holidays

Jan. 1 – New Year's Day
Jan. 15 – Coming of Age Day
Feb. 11 – National Foundation Day
Mar. 21 – Vernal Equinox Day
Apr. 29 – Greenery Day to honor
former emperor Hirohito's
birthday
May 3 – Constitution Day
May 5 – Children's Day
Sep. 15 – Respect for the Aged Day
Sep. 23 – Autumnal Equinox Day
Oct. 10 – Health and Sport Day
Nov. 3 – Culture Day
Nov. 23 – Labor Thanksgiving
Dec. 23 – Emperor Akihito's birthday

The snow festival at Sapporo

For children

The star festival is celebrated on the seventh night of the seventh month (July 7). Children write poems and tie the papers to bamboo branches.

Girls age 7 and 3, and boys 5 years old have a special day in November. November 15 is called *Shichi-go-san* (7-5-3). The children dress in kimonos or their best clothes and go to shrines to pray for good health. March 3 is Girl's Day. Daughters in each home display sets of dolls dressed in court clothes. The end of winter is marked in February by throwing beans and shouting *oni wa soto, fuku wa uchi*, which means "go out devils, come in good luck."

Children dressed in traditional kimonos for a festival

Religion

The most popular religions in Japan are Shinto and Buddhism. Many Japanese follow both religions. Babies and marriages are blessed at Shinto shrines and funerals are held in Buddhist temples.

Shinto

Shinto is the oldest religion in Japan. The name means "the way of the gods." Shinto gods are in the sun, trees and mountains. The highest mountain in Japan is Mount Fuji. The tenth emperor, Suijin, built a shrine to the goddess of volcanoes on the northern slopes of Mount Fuji. He hoped this would make people less afraid of volcanoes. Mount Fuji last erupted nearly 300 years ago, but there are about 80 active volcanoes in Japan.

A Shinto shrine is a place of calm and beauty. Most Japanese aim to visit the shrine at Ise at least once in their lives.

A red torii, or gateway, separates the shrine from the rest of the world. Stone animals guard the entrance. There is a special place to wash the hands and a type of wooden box to throw coins into as offerings. Visitors can read their fortunes on pieces of paper. If the fortune is not good, the paper is tied to a tree to leave the bad luck behind.

The emperor

Japanese legends say that the first emperor of Japan was Jimmu, the great-grandson of the sun goddess. Until about 50 years ago many Japanese still believed the emperor was also a god. In 1946 Emperor Hirohito officially announced that he was not a god but just a symbol of the state and of the unity of the people.

The torii at Itukushima Shrine, Hiroshima

A "dragon dance" at a Buddhist temple

Buddhism

Buddhists pray in a temple before a statue of Buddha, an Indian prince who taught his followers how to cope with suffering. Buddhism came to Japan from China and Korea about 1,500 years ago. Buddhist monks showed the Japanese how to write using Chinese characters. After about 400 years a group of Zen Buddhist monks brought new ideas to Japan. Zen Buddhists practice quiet thinking, or meditation, and self-control. Zen monks introduced the tea ceremony and the idea of rock gardens as a place to meditate. The tea ceremony combines Shinto and Buddhist beliefs. It lasts about four hours. Zen monks believe tea opens their minds for meditation.

Confucius

Confucius, or K'ung fu-tzu, was a teacher and writer who lived in China from 551 B.C. to 478 B.C. His wise words have been widely read ever since. About 2,000 years ago, his teaching on the importance of the group rather than the individual became popular in Japan. Many Japanese still read and follow the ideas of Confucius.

Christianity

One of the first foreigners to visit Japan was a Spanish priest, St. Francis Xavier. He came to Japan in 1549. During the next 100 years, his followers, a Christian group called Jesuits, converted 500,000 Japanese people to Christianity. Then Christianity was banned for nearly 300 years. Today there are about one million Japanese who follow the Christian faith.

The Buddha at Todaiji Temple, Nara

Japan at war

In the 1860s Japan was forced to open up to the outside world and quickly became an industrial nation. Less than 30 years later, a Japanese army went to war with another country for the first time in Japanese history. The Japanese now needed raw materials, such as oil, for industry and also more people to sell goods to. They fought their nearest neighbors, the Chinese. The war with China began in 1894. The countries were fighting to gain power over Korea. China was a much bigger country than Japan, so people were surprised when Japan won.

Ten years later, Japan declared war on its other near neighbor, Russia. This time the argument was about Manchuria, which is on the mainland of Asia and has a border with Russia. Japan wanted Manchuria's soybeans, iron ore and coal.

The Russians did not want the Japanese so close to their border. Again the Japanese won.

World War II

Japan had become a world power and now controlled land outside its own islands. The population of Japan was growing fast, and there was not enough space to house and feed all the people. The American government stopped Japanese people from moving to the United States. This caused a lot of anger in Japan. In 1941 the Japanese entered World War II when they bombed the American fleet at Pearl Harbor in the Pacific. Fighting went on for four years.

A view of the damage to the city of Hiroshima after the atomic bomb exploded. The building on the right has been preserved as a memorial.

Self-Defense Forces on parade

The first atomic bomb

The Japanese earned a reputation for "fanatical resistance" during World War II. The war ended only after two American atomic bombs were dropped on Japan. The bomb that exploded over the city of Hiroshima on August 6, 1945, killed 78,000 people. Over 30,000 people suffered horrible injuries. On August 9 another bomb killed 45,000 people in Nagasaki. American planes dropped three million leaflets over Japan asking the people to persuade their emperor to surrender and end the war. On August 15, Japan did surrender.

Okinawa

The only fighting in Japan during World War II was on Okinawa. In three months, near the end of the war, 50,000 Americans and 110,000 Japanese soldiers died there. So did one third of the population of Okinawa, many from disease. The U.S. government kept Okinawa as a military base until 1972. Now Okinawa is part of Japan again.

Occupation

For the first time in Japanese history, Japan had been conquered by foreigners. Soldiers and advisers, mainly Americans, stayed in Japan until 1952. They helped the Japanese rebuild their industry. Changes were made to the constitution, affecting the rules about how the country is governed.

Self-Defense Forces

Part of the constitution of Japan says that Japanese people will never use force in any conflict outside Japan. There is no army, but Japan does train soldiers. They belong to the Self-Defense Forces. In June 1992, the Japanese parliament passed a new law. Up to 2,000 Japanese soldiers can now work with the United Nations outside Japan, but they must not fight.

An antinuclear protest march

A changing world

A technician working at NADSA's Space Center, in Isukuba

In just one century, Japan changed completely. The nation had been cut off from the rest of the world. Now Japan depends on world trade more than any other country. It needs to buy raw materials, energy and food from abroad. Japan earns the money for these imports by developing new technologies and new products to make and sell at home and abroad.

New markets

Nearly half of Japan's trade is with North America, Europe and Australia, but the Japanese are looking for new markets for their goods. They spend a lot of money setting up factories in other countries. Goods may be produced more cheaply abroad than in Japan, where costs are high. In return for money, jobs and technology, the Japanese expect to sell more of their goods in these countries. In Great Britain nearly half the new cars are Japanese models, while in Thailand almost every new car bought is Japanese.

Old people pray at a Tokyo temple

An aging population

Japanese people can expect to live longer than any other group in the world. Most men live to around 76 years and women to 82. More married women now have jobs and fewer children. Smaller families mean there will soon be more old people than young in Japan. The old people are known as the silver generation. Few people are unemployed in Japan. As the older people retire, there may not be enough young people to support and look after them.

Aid for land

The Japanese have also swapped aid for land. There are 47,000 Russians living on the Kuril Islands, off the coast of Hokkaido. The Japanese have agreed to give Russia money and help with technology if two of the Kuril Islands are returned to Japan.

Whaling

In the past, Japan had the largest whaling fleet in the world. If they were allowed to do so, modern Japanese whaling boats could catch as many as 37 whales a day. However, since there is a ban on killing whales, whaling bases like the Ogasawara Islands are now becoming tourist centers for watching whales.

The space race

The Japanese only entered the space race in 1970. The first rockets launched from the site on Tanegashima Island were made from American designs. Now U.S. rocket makers are buying Japanese engines.

The Japanese scientist Yoji Ishikawa thinks that "by the year 2057 there will be 150 Japanese settlers living on Mars."

A satellite launch at Osaki

Fact file

Government

Ever since the shoguns lost power, the emperors of Japan have reigned but not ruled. Instead, the Japanese looked abroad for ideas and planned a new system of government to replace the shoguns. They chose a parliament to make laws, like the one in Great Britain. The parliament is called the Diet. There are over 700 members of the Diet. They belong to either the House of Councillors (252 members) or the House of Representatives. Politicians are elected to the House of Councillors for six years or to the House of Representatives for four years. Each house has 16 committees. Committee members meet to discuss special problems. Members of the Diet choose the prime minister. The prime minister chooses 20 people for the cabinet.

Flag

The national flag of Japan is white with a red circle in the center. The circle is a symbol for the sun. The Chinese first called Japan Nihon. *Ni* means "sun" and *hon* is "source"— the "land of the rising sun." The name Japan came from a European traveler, Marco Polo, 700 years ago.

The emperor's flag has a gold chrysanthemum in the middle of it.

National anthem

The national anthem is "Kimigayo," which means "His Majesty's Reign." The words are from a thousand-year-old poem. It was first sung to music on the emperor's birthday in 1880.

Religion

Over 100 million people in Japan follow Shinto, and 91 million say they are Buddhist. This is more than the total population of Japan (124 million). Most Japanese people believe in both Shinto and Buddhism.

Money

The Japanese currency is the yen. The name comes from a Chinese word meaning "round" and "a dollar." The sign is written ¥.

Education

All Japanese children go to elementary school for six years and then to junior high school for three years. Most pupils go to senior high school for three years. More than two million students study at universities. There are more than 500 universities in Japan. Most are private.

Newspapers and television

The main national newspapers are published each day in Tokyo and are sold all over Japan. There are also four daily newspapers in English and a weekly paper with financial news.

Nearly all Japanese homes have at least one color television set. Viewers in Tokyo have the biggest choice of programs.

Some famous people

Japanese names have the surname first.

Murasaki Shikibu (978?-1014?) wrote *The Tale of Genji*, one of the world's first novels. She was a lady-in-waiting to the empress

Katsushika Hokusai (1760-1849) was an artist whose prints and drawings made the Japanese style popular in Europe

Iwasaki Yataro (1835-85) founded the giant company Mitsubishi

Ito Hirobumi (1841-1909) was Japan's first prime minister after the Meiji Restoration

Kano Jigoro (1860-1938) developed the sport of judo

Yamamato Isoroku (1884-1943) was the naval leader who planned and directed the attack on Pearl Harbor

Ichikawa Fusae (1893-1981) led the campaign for women to have the right to vote in Japan

Suzuki Shin'ichi (1898-) started an education movement. Now 300,000 children around the world follow his method of learning to play the violin

Hirohito Michinomiya (1901-89) became the 124th emperor of Japan in 1926

Tomonaga Shin'ichiro (1906-) won the Nobel Prize for physics in 1965

Kurosawa Akira (1910-) is an internationally known film director

Mishima Yukio (1925-70) wrote plays, novels and essays

Chiyonofuji (1955-) held the top rank in sumo wrestling for 10 years

Miyake Issey (1938-) has shown his fashion designs in Paris for over 20 years

Some key events in history

A.D. 400s: contacts between peoples of China and Japan. The most powerful Japanese clans united to form the Yamato state

710: first capital built at Nara

794: capital moved to Heian-kyo (Kyoto). Beginning of the Heian period

1185: Yoritomo won war between rival clans and became military ruler of Japan. He was given the title shogun

1542: first contact with the West, when Portuguese sailors arrived with guns

1549: St. Francis Xavier introduced Christianity to Japan

1603: Tokugawa Ieyasu became the first of many shoguns from the Tokugawa family and made Edo his capital

1616-1853: Edo period. Japan cut off from the rest of the world

1853: United States ships arrived off the coast of Japan with their commander, Matthew Perry

1858: Japan opened some ports to foreign ships and signed trade agreements

1868: military rule by the shoguns ended and the emperor moved to Edo, renamed Tokyo

1894: war with China

1904: war with Russia

1941: Japan supported the Germans in World War II and bombed the American fleet at Pearl Harbor

1945: Japan surrendered after atomic bombs were dropped on Hiroshima and Nagasaki

1952: end of occupation of Japan by U.S. and Allied forces

1956: Japan joined the United Nations

Index

Ainu 10
arts 12, 13

baseball 15, 19
boats 9
Buddhism 12, 16, 24, 25, 30
bullet trains 9
Bunraku 13

cars 8, 20, 21, 28
children 7, 16, 18, 19, 23, 30
Christianity 25, 31
climate 5, 20, 21
Confucius 25

emperors 10, 11, 12, 13, 19, 24, 27, 30, 31
energy 21, 28

farming 20-21
festivals 22, 23
fishing 13, 20, 21
flag 30
food 16, 17

gifts 7
government 10, 11, 13, 27, 30

Hirohito (emperor) 23, 24, 31
Hiroshima 20, 21, 24, 26, 27, 31
Hokkaido 5, 9, 10, 21, 22, 29
holidays 22, 23
Honshu 5, 9, 20, 21
housing 14

industry 12, 19, 20, 21, 26, 27

Japan Airlines (JAL) 9
Japanese Alps 5, 22
juku 19

kana 6, 7
kanji 6, 7
karaoke 15
Kyoto 10, 11, 12, 13
Kyushu 5, 20, 21

language 6

martial arts 19
Mount Fuji 9, 24

Nagasaki 21, 27, 31
national anthem 30
ninja 19

Okinawa 27
Osaka 9

pachinko 15
pollution 20

railroads 8-9
religion 12, 24, 25, 30
robots 20

schools 15, 18, 19, 22, 30
Sea of Japan 5
Seikan Tunnel 9
Self-Defense Forces 27
Shikoku 5, 9
Shinto 12, 15, 24, 25, 30
shoguns 11, 13, 19, 30, 31
shopping 7, 17
skiing 22
sports 14-15, 18, 19
sumo wrestling 15, 31

temples 10, 12, 24, 25, 29
theater 13
Tokyo 5, 6, 8, 9, 12, 13, 15, 17, 18, 29, 30, 31
transportation 8-9

volcanoes 24

whaling 29
women 6, 10, 13, 19
World War II 13, 14, 26, 27, 31
writing 7, 12, 25

Yokohama 13